MW00667684

Praise for *the* LEGACY CONVERSATION

"Too often, families spend the vast majority of their efforts on passing the tangible elements on to their heirs. The truly successful families are able to pass on their intangibles and these are the "assets" that span generations. This book is a great guide to begin these powerful and important discussions."

> - David Filkin - Principal, Gresham Partners, LLC

"As an advisor to wealthy families, I read many books and articles and often attend conferences on wealth management. Without fail, the subject matter focuses on money. This book is a must-read for anyone who distinguishes tangible assets from intangibles within a truly intentional legacy plan."

> - George C. Weir - Senior Vice President & Manager - Trust Division
> First Hawaiian Bank

"The true legacy that families present to the next generation is not about the monetary inheritance, although this is often the focal point of the next generation, it is the cohesion of the family and the passing of its values. This book addresses that and thus is very valuable to our supporters and their children."

> - Michael C. Cleavenger - V.P. Fund Development,
> La Rabida Children's Hospital

"I have always encouraged financial advisors to re-focus on creating deeper emotional connections with their clients, preached the nobility of our profession as we seek to build and fund client goals. Further, I encourage them to meet the "holistic" needs of their clients, not just portfolio construction. In this ground breaking work I discovered there actually is a process to do all that and more."

> - Anthony J. DiLeonardi - Vice Chairman,
> Guggenheim Funds Distributors, Inc.

the LEGACY
CONVERSATION
the missing gem in wealth planning

2ND EDITION

Carolyn J. Friend, Psy.D & James M. Weiner, Psy.D

ADLER & FOREST MEDIA

The *Inheriting Wisdom* Legacy Wheel © 2008 by Adler & Forest, LLC

Book Cover Designed by Rubidium Design
© Veer Incorporated - AYP1501186

Second Edition: October 2010
Published by:
Adler & Forest Media

Printed in the United States of America

Library of Congress Cataloging-in-Publication Data

Friend, Carolyn J.
  The legacy conversation : the missing gem in wealth planning / Carolyn J. Friend & James M. Weiner. -- 2nd ed.

     p. : ill. ; cm.

  Spec. 1st ed. published: Oconomowoc, WI : MavenMark Books, 2010.
  ISBN: 978-0-615-40489-9

  1. Finance, Personal. 2. Legacies. 3. Wealth. I. Weiner, James M. II. Title.

HG179 .F75 2010
332.024/016   2010937397

To our parents,
Sol and Malkie Friend
and
Rabbi Karl and Eva Weiner,
who passed to us their very best seeds of wisdom
as we grew our own garden.
May their memories be for a blessing.

CONTENTS

the LEGACY
CONVERSATION
the missing gem in wealth planning

PREFACE

In 2003, certain life events led Carolyn and me to make a professional course correction, ultimately resulting in the creation of *Inheriting Wisdom: The Legacy Process That Reaches Across Generations.* In retrospect, we can easily identify the personal and professional experiences that sustained us through the process of taking an idea from concept to product. Neither of us predicted what it was going to take to develop the Gen-T Legacy Institute, the business that would bring our intellectual capital to market. But we would both tell you that *The Legacy Conversation* will alter families' lives and change how we conceptualize wealth so that future generations can experience the robust benefits of legacy planning.

When we embarked on our new path, the objective seemed simple: address the regret frequently expressed with the phrase "If only we'd had a chance to talk about…" Specifically, families seldom set aside time to have open conversations about their wisdom: their guiding principles and beliefs, family culture and traditions, and life experiences.

Many of us mistakenly assume that simply living in close proximity to our families, having parents as role models, and even documenting our values in family mission statements and ethical wills for the next generation all serve to counteract any "if only" regrets. While all three ways help the generations connect, do they encourage family members to build confidence in the significance of their own voices within the family? Though they certainly help to build memories, even family trips with our adult children don't guarantee that we have created an environment for focused dialogue.

The handwriting in the background of the book cover comes from a page in the journal written by my father, Rabbi Karl Weiner, on his voyage to "Amerika." Twenty-five years after my father's death, my mother finally relinquished control over all the family memorabilia stored in their basement. My parents would have rejected being referred to as Holocaust survivors since they weren't in the camps. But given the contents of this journal and other documents from their days in Germany, and in light of the way they were hidden away, it's hard to find a better term for their experiences.

Overwhelmed with the prospect of going through decades of their history, Carolyn's and my plan was to declutter the house first. Then we'd move slowly to where the pictures, documents, books, and writing were stored in the basement. As you'll read about in Chapter 1, Carolyn had undertaken this same task after the death of her parents.

Reaching up to the top of one of the basement shelves, above some old paint cans and aged journals, we found a beaten-up green box. My parents' riches had sat for decades on that shelf. Along with the difficult-to-obtain visas and passports that allowed them to find their way out of Germany in 1939 were two gems.

The first, an album of photos taken on a Leica camera, documented their trip by boat from Dresden, through England, to what was then called Palestine. In red ink on blue paper, in German, was the poetry my father had written to his in-laws. Along with the photographs, it gave a glimpse of their lives as they were forced to travel far away from their home. After digitally restoring the pictures and having the German translated, it was hard to avoid a sense of regret: "If only they were alive, we could have a chance to talk about…"

Far less dramatic in presentation, the second gem was a journal written on another voyage. Again, my father wanted to capture his experiences, but this time the purpose was private and personal. Every entry in his chronicle radiated enthusiasm. Repeatedly restricted from direct passage to the United States, my parents were forced to route themselves through India. Even the conditions of their travel were blurred by the promise of the freedom and opportunity that lay ahead. No doubt it was this vision that sustained my parents through their voyage. A similar vision of freedom and opportunity was presented to me and our youngest daughter, Ivy, at the Newseum in Washington, DC. This interactive museum brings to life the power of our free press and the uniqueness of our country, "Amerika."

Even though no bloodlines connect our politically minded daughter and my father (she being his step-grandchild), Carolyn and I could imagine the conversation that would have taken place between them regarding these precious ideals, had he still been alive. We felt the kinship; no family mission or values statement could have been as powerful in bridging the generations. After all, we are the link connecting their experiences.

Shortly after Carolyn and I married, we were pulled in several directions by the increasing need to care for our aging parents, to define and grow ourselves professionally, and to do our best to parent a blended family. We were part of what the media at the time popularized as the "sandwich generation." The image of being squished like peanut butter between the demands of two other generations never worked for either of us.

As difficult as those years were, we both measure our accomplishments to date by how we faced the challenges. We are both professional clinical psychologists. No doubt our backgrounds contributed a great deal to our creating *Inheriting Wisdom*, but the idea's substance comes from the seeds of wisdom left to us by our parents. Watching our children live their lives, we can only hope that each of them makes the best use of our seeds of wisdom as they tend to their own gardens.

The Legacy Conversation expresses the concepts we've worked on over the years. Our approach is straightforward: create a process that guides family members to discover their own wisdom, and figure out the best way to reach across the generation gap.

The logic of tackling these two issues seemed obvious to us, until we were struck by how rapid the pace of change has been during our lifetimes. We needed to go no further than Carolyn's father's experience in order to recognize the shift in thinking we were suggesting.

At the end of World War II, Carolyn's father, Sol, returned from Egypt. About to marry, he needed a way to support himself and the family that was soon to come. When he heard about a machine that offered a unique process for packaging food, he went to see it in action. Taking a calculated risk, he invested in the machine and began producing buttered beefsteaks.

Those were not easy years, but he signed his name to the bottom line and pursued his goals. Carolyn's mother and father managed the production, a romantic beginning to a long life together. Of course, her father found himself operating as both marketing and sales departments. From selling store to store in the beginning, his business grew to having a national presence. Without wavering, he kept his eye on providing for his family.

Sol prided himself on being level headed and pragmatic. Common sense was his teacher. Sol's children understood that his long hours and hard work were about providing for the family. It was always clear that money was for practical purposes and the needs of the family. However, when it came time for discussions about money, the door closed. These talks were for the accountant's ears only. Carolyn's mother was, generally speaking, not a part of those discussions. For Sol's generation, managing money was a man's way of protecting his wife and family.

In contrast to his guarded approach to family money matters, business was discussed openly at the dinner table, and Carolyn's mother, May, was Sol's most respected advisor. By listening to the conversations held during meals, the family learned about the importance of making thoughtful decisions and about the priority of taking care of those who work for you. Sol was serious about his responsibilities.

Carolyn's father was a man's man and the patriarch of the family; everyone knew he was the boss. His approach was common for men of his generation. His competitiveness fueled his desire to be successful. Prosperity was equal to winning. This kept him forging ahead. It was never solely about wealth. But we know the world has changed and modern-day entrepreneurs, as well as the inheritors of the previous generation's wealth, tend to approach life and family differently.

Our vision is to create a means for families to talk about the "if only" questions while the opportunity exists. We do not know if our fathers would have welcomed this kind of conversation, but we are finding it increasingly clear that younger generations want this discussion, so much so that they are willing to invite their parents and grandparents to the table.

As our idea crystallized, we began our foray into the marketplace in order to test reactions, to learn as much as we could. Not surprisingly, the biggest question we faced was, "How are you going to get accomplished men who are used to taking control, to being the 'boss,' to commit time for this kind of activity?" The assumption was that being results-oriented, bottom-line kinds of guys, "They are going to want to know what they are going to get out of it."

Some people over the last forty to fifty years have addressed these concerns by promoting the development of "family mission statements" and endorsing family governance. The impetus has been to focus on the transitioning of tangibles, such as a family business or the family's accumulated wealth. We know that many family members have spent their lives in the shadow of a family business, or as part of an affluent family. In this regard, creating a conversation about wisdom and how to pass it down, while pushing the conversation about money to the side for the time being is, for many, unfamiliar territory.

In the wake of the economic tsunami of the last few years, more people now realize how fragile it is to count on the tangibles to get one through life. The future holds unknown risks, some of which we can begin to chart and others that remain uncharted. Our experience has been that what holds everything together for families, the "sticky," is all about transferring our intangibles.

The Legacy Conversation, while acknowledging some of the specific challenges that come with affluence, recognizes that *everyone* has a legacy. It is the wisdom contained in this legacy that is an essential component of an enduring heritage. Of course, intentional legacy planning must also address financial, philanthropic, and legal concerns. Figuring out how to pass on cherished possessions, as well as how to manage the medical and life concerns of a family, must be addressed. Wisdom serves as the driving force in assuring a holistic approach to creating an enduring legacy.

*We transfer our full wealth, meaningfully and wisely,
by incorporating our intangible and tangible legacy.*

CHAPTER 1
Your Legacy and What Really Matters

I stared I could not move. It was overwhelming. I said to myself; "Carolyn, this is all that's left." Framed photographs, high school yearbooks, a letter sweater, clothes, shoes, purses, and little mementos all carefully gathered and placed in neat piles. I stood there. My parents had just passed away, 35 days apart from each other. This had been their home. Although filled with furniture, clothing, and other personal items, their home felt lifeless. As the eldest daughter, it was my responsibility to clear out the house. (Of course, if I were the eldest son, I would have managed the finances.)

As I handled each item, my recollections made me smile and at times laugh. Sorting through the possessions, I thought about my parents and pondered all that they gave us. Then I realized that the gifts were really bits of wisdom, and they were everywhere, embedded in objects, memories, and stories, often funny stories. Imagine if, while my parents were alive, there had been a way for them to consciously pass along their wisdom. Sadly, an opportunity had been missed.

Like most families, mine communicated guiding principles and beliefs, family culture and traditions, enduring insights, and wisdom—but in silence. We make plans to bequeath our tangibles, especially money and cherished possessions, to those important to us. But the gateway to passing on that which enables us to thrive in rapidly changing times remains closed.

Tangibles constitute only half of our wealth. Creating a plan to pass on our intangibles is crucial.

The key is to begin by entering into conversations with our family members and those important to us about the subtle and more abstract parts of our legacy. Then we will be transferring our full wealth, meaningfully and wisely.

The intangible part of our legacy contains "what matters"—those things we know and use when making decisions. It is that which guides us as we face life's challenges. It is the place where our wisdom lives and grows. So let us have a candid conversation.

What mark will we leave on the world? What defines how we will be remembered? Perhaps others will think of us and recall the money, jewelry, and art we gave to family members, or the business we created, or a plaque bearing our name that recognizes our time and treasure given to a favorite charitable institution. These gifts are concrete and can be quantified. Each of us spends 99 percent of our estate-planning time on our tangible legacy, creating trusts, wills, and financial plans. We invest this time, personally as well as with trusted advisors, with the belief that within those documents lies our lasting legacy.

However, these constitute only half of our wealth. Creating a plan to pass on our intangibles is also crucial, if it is our intention to formulate an enduring legacy.

The Key to Creating a Lasting Legacy

We ponder: What is the most important thing we can bequeath to our families? What can we give them as a guide when they face difficult decisions in life? We rightly believe that the solid foundation is made up of our family culture and traditions, our guiding principles and beliefs.

Our wisdom resides in the intangible parts of our lives, in our thoughts and in the outworking of those thoughts. We are aware of its presence. It influences our reasoning and our approach to life as we handle life's demands. For most of us it is "just there," and we use it without fanfare. Our legacy is powered by wisdom.

> **Think about the decisions you make daily. What are some of the guiding principles you apply?**

Wisdom is the integration of our family traditions and culture, our guiding principles and beliefs, and our life experiences. By passing on our seeds of wisdom, we strengthen and connect generations.

Everyone has wisdom, and it is personal. We each define and characterize wisdom uniquely. Wisdom is our inner resourcefulness. We acquire it, and when making a decision, we draw upon it. In the face of life's challenges, it is resilient and enduring.

Wisdom can be defined as the integration of our family traditions and culture, our guiding principles and beliefs, and our life experiences. Wisdom can be articulated. By passing on the exceptional seeds, we strengthen and connect generations with our knowledge and insights.

Think of our lives as gardens. Each of us has a personal plot of land. We begin creating our garden by planting the seeds of wisdom given to us from the generations that came before. We cultivate our garden. In the process, we decide where we want to live and what careers we will pursue, among the many life actions we take.

Then along comes the next generation. They look at the garden and say, "I'm on Twitter®. The guru says you should move this plant over here, and this one over there. As a matter of fact, you should just let me take over."

But it is our garden. Among the things it contains are our knowledge and insights. We don't want to hand control over to the next generation just yet. We know they need life experiences. As previous generations have done, we choose only the best seeds of wisdom and pass them along.

The act of transferring our seeds of wisdom is an essential component of our legacy. When shared, wisdom empowers those important to us to prevail when dealing with life's puzzles.

Passing on wisdom is an intentional act. Avoid the common lament, "They just won't listen." Conversations are one of the most successful techniques for passing along wisdom. We must engage others in a way that stimulates *their* thinking. Be purposeful. Be clear. Know the boundaries, since naturally we will meet resistance. By being thoughtful about our garden's design, we can pass the very best seeds on to the next generation and begin creating a lasting legacy.

A friend once told us about a conversation he had with his son regarding a vintage Fender Stratocaster (a famous electric guitar model). His 14-year-old asked if eventually he would be given the Strat. Since his message was intentional, the father chose his words carefully: "This guitar has a long history. My father helped me pick it out.

> When approaching those important to you, have they welcomed or resisted your wisdom?

It was Leo Fender's unique design that helped redefine the electric guitar. Of course, you already know that. You also know I love playing it. You will find your passion, whether it is music, painting, or poetry. Then we will work together to get the instrument or tools you need."

This story reveals the father's wisdom about finding an artistic outlet for his son. The father knows from life experience that working at playing the guitar brought him a sense of fulfillment. He wants the same for his son. But he is wise enough to know that, for his son, fulfillment may or may not come through the guitar. This story is about family support, something that is intangible. It is about the father's wisdom.

**

I am back in my parents' empty house, sitting at the kitchen table, looking at their personal items. I remember one incident that speaks of my father's wisdom. My father, also a businessman, would come home from work and talk about his daily experi-

Wisdom is our inner resourcefulness. We acquire it, and when making a decision, we draw upon it. In the face of life's challenges, it is resilient and enduring.

ences. One day, he told us about a call he received from a company that had represented his product for thirty years. It was the owner's son calling him for business advice. Always willing to share, Dad spoke with the caller at length. His answers were thoughtful, forthright, and direct, consistent with his reputation in business and how he dealt with life.

Seeds of wisdom like those my dad passed on to others come from ancestors and life experiences. They live in the intangibles and in our memories. Wisdom is an essential component of our legacy, and it is vital that we convey it to those important to us. We must do so in a thoughtful and forthright manner to pass along our full wealth meaningfully and wisely.

We wish to share the best of our gardens, as parents to children or to those important to us. Then we hope they will take those seeds and make their own gardens, build their own lives.

CHAPTER 2
A Deeper Longing

"Reputation is everything!" The saying is universal. Leaving a good name is a crucial part of a deep longing to leave our mark on the next generation.

Easy Eddie

If you read the widely distributed e-mail about "Easy Eddie," Al Capone's infamous attorney, you would understand. What else can explain the intense emotional responses, even tears, from those who learned about his unexpected actions? He wanted to guarantee the legacy of a "good name" for his son, a longing that resonates with all of us.

In a blaze of gunfire, Easy Eddie met his death on a lonely Chicago street in 1939. Given Eddie's association with the Chicago mob, as well as his previous life choices, this murder

The clock of life is wound but once
And no man has the power
To tell just when the hands will stop
At late or early hour....
Now is the only time you own.
Live, love, toil with a will.
Place no faith in time
For the clock may soon be still.

—Robert H. Smith (1932)

came as no surprise. What was a surprise was finding in his pocket a crumpled page, torn from a magazine, with the words of this poem. Violent death is tragic, but knowing the trail of victims left by the Chicago organization, it's likely that many people wished Capone had died along with Easy Eddie that night. Some believe that Capone ordered this assassination as his revenge for betrayal. What actually happened? A year earlier Easy Eddie had provided the authorities with the information needed to put Capone behind bars for tax evasion.

Besides being Capone's attorney, Easy Eddie had been the mobster's friend and confidant. He was a skilled jurist who had kept Capone out of jail for a long time. His importance to the organization was evident. The mere size of his bonuses suggested his stature in the mob. For his services, Eddie was given protection and a piece of the action. He lived in a fenced mansion that covered an entire city block. No doubt all the benefits of the high life were his. It's clear that he was more than a hireling. He was fully aware of the atrocities perpetrated by the mobsters, and he did not care.

Eddie's one soft spot was his son, whom he loved dearly. No expense was spared to make sure his son could have the best. Fine clothes, a car, and the best education that money could buy were all provided for this young man.

Easy Eddie also tried to teach his son the difference between right and wrong. He hoped that his son would end up a better man than he. But ultimately, he recognized that with all his wealth and influence, there were two things he could not buy for his son: a good name and a good example.

In spite of his role in the Chicago, organization, Eddie was driven to try to change his reputation, especially for his son. Thus he approached the revenue authorities and revealed the truth about Capone.

He knew his testimony would come at great personal cost. But Eddie's consolation was knowing that he was giving his son the greatest gift he had to offer at the greatest price he could ever pay. While he couldn't

Easy Eddie recognized that with all his wealth and influence, there were two things he could not buy for his son: a good name and a good example.

change the past, he hoped this moment of integrity would become his legacy.

Butch O'Hare

The same e-mail told about a Chicago hero, World War II Lieutenant Commander Butch O'Hare. In Chicago, the international airport is named in his honor.

Butch was stationed in the South Pacific as a member of a team of six Wildcat fighters whose mother ship was the *USS Lexington.* The *Lexington* had been assigned the dangerous task of penetrating enemy-held waters to make a strike at Japanese shipping. Unfortunately, while still 400 miles from her destination, she was discovered by the Japanese. Nine bombers were sent to destroy the *Lexington,* but they were successfully repelled.

In the meantime, an additional nine Japanese bombers were on their way. Six Wildcats, one piloted by O'Hare, roared off the *Lexington*'s deck to stop them. He and his wingman were the first to spot the bombers, but the other Wildcats were too far away to reach the enemy planes and release their bombs. As if this weren't bad enough, O'Hare's wingman discovered his guns were jammed. He was forced to turn away. Butch O'Hare flew alone between the *Lexington* and the bombers.

As the e-mail dramatically put it, "Laying aside all thoughts of personal safety, he dove into the formation of Japanese planes." The description continues, "Wing-mounted .50 calibers blazed as he charged in." Even when Butch's ammunition was spent, he dove and maneuvered, attempting to make the enemy fighters retreat.

After he returned to the *Lexington*, the movie cameras attached to his plane confirmed that Butch O'Hare had downed five Japanese fighters, damaging a sixth. Single-handedly, he had protected the carrier. Risking his life for the safety of others, he received the first Congressional Medal of Honor in World War II "for conspicuous gallantry and intrepidity in aerial combat."

His navy career was filled with valiant acts, but on November 27, 1943, Butch was killed in battle. He was 29. His plane went down, and his body was never found.

The Real Question

The e-mail echoed our thoughts: "What do these two men have in common?"

Imagine our surprise to find out that Edward Henry "Butch" O'Hare was Edward J. "Easy Eddie" O'Hare's son!

Eddie's act of courage in risking everything by turning on Capone set off bells for many of us: we believe his story, and we identify with his desire to leave a good legacy. We share the same longing and intuitively recognize that our legacy, our real affluence, our wisdom, is what we desire to pass on.

Money empowers, but without wisdom, our plans, even with the guidance of the best of advisors, are at risk. Our longing for connection, not the things we give, explains our resonance with the father/son story of Easy Eddie and Butch O'Hare.

Notorious mob lawyer Easy Eddie O'Hare teaches his son Butch the value of honesty and integrity; the son goes on to become a decorated war hero and dies in the service of his country.

We believe it meant that Eddie got the message to consider his impact on others—or at the very least, on his beloved son. Briefly, reality was suspended. Ignoring all we know about people who are "fully aware of the atrocities of the mob," we still hoped Eddie O'Hare's deepest longing moved him to change. Most of all, we wished that loving Butch had melted his cold heart.

"The legacy of heroes is the memory of a great name and the inheritance of a great example."

— Benjamin Disraeli, 19th Century British politician

The Desired Conversation

As if it were yesterday, I remember the day my father, Rabbi Karl Weiner, died. I was 30 years old. So much remained unspoken between us. It seemed strange to me at the time, even in the midst of my grief, that as a rabbi, he spent his life having purposeful conversations with so many. I was convinced that he had helped all my friends open up with their parents. Why had he not opened up with me?

Why couldn't we find a way to have a dialogue? I longed for this connection even after his death. One day, long after his passing, I stood in front of his headstone, talking to him. If only this conversation could have occurred when he was alive.

We all have disappointments. Imagine what doors we could have opened had we gotten past our father-son annoyances. Our words would have been substantive—talking about what really matters, about the intangibles. We could have discussed:

- *Our guiding principles*
- *Our thoughts about family culture and traditions*
- *Our paths to spirituality or our higher sense of meaning*
- *Our ways of finding well-being*
- *Our feelings about our accomplishments*

When I became a step-parent of three, I, too, felt awkward initiating these conversations. Over time, I've come to realize that the hardest part was getting started.

We all wish to share the best of our gardens, as parents to children or to those important to us. Then we hope they will take those seeds and make their own gardens, build their own lives. Perhaps give us grandchildren. But even if they don't, we hope that in this rapidly changing world, the members of the next generation will cultivate their gardens and find ways to pass on their choicest seeds, thus leaving their marks on the world.

Legacy is the simple notion that what we do today will shine its light throughout and beyond our lifetime.

It's Not Magic

Naturally, before we shared the tale of Eddie and Butch, we decided to confirm the authenticity of the story.

We realized that Eddie's sudden change in behavior was out of character. Evidence exists that he desired to do the best for his son; perhaps he worried about the effect of his reputation on his son's life. But there was no magic moment.

If we look beyond the folklore portrayed in the e-mail, we're left with a far more realistic picture. *Collier's* magazine in 1947 made public Eddie O'Hare's role as an informant. Whatever his wishes for his son, one thing is certain: no great moment of conscience single-handedly motivated a "magic" change of character. Easy Eddie had been and remained an informant for some time.

On the other hand, Butch deserved his good name. He was a popular leader. Demanding a level of excellence from the

Legacy is the simple notion that what we do today will shine its light throughout and beyond our lifetime.

pilots under him, he worked hard. He also enjoyed swimming and spear fishing, often taking his squadron with him and cooking the catch. With an unassuming personality, Edward Henry insisted his men call him "Butch." The exact details of the heroic day vary slightly in different accounts, but no doubt exists that this young man put his personal safety at risk to ensure the safety of the *Lexington* and the American fleet.

Change Requires Intention

Recently we were privileged to interview the fourth generation descendant of the founder of a 100-year-old family manufacturing business. We will refer to him as Mark Black. Sustaining a family-owned business over ten decades is no small feat.

Mark has a passion for organizational renewal. He commented, "I am always at my peak when I am in a steep learning curve."

In a renowned business magazine, Mark tells a story of corporate revitalization, noting, "We were financially conservative and placed great emphasis on integrity in business and on product quality." His experience as a board member during a period of transition has contributed to his current consulting efforts.

Our conversation with Mark was rich. His passion for renewal, both professionally and personally, came alive as we talked. We were flattered and touched when Mark "turned the pages of his life story," giving us an intimate glimpse of his private world.

He had been taken care of by governesses, and provided the opportunity to attend the best boarding schools. These benefited Mark in many ways, but didn't prevent him from feeling that he was a "visitor" at home, starting at the age of 14, because, as Mark said, "my dad had no idea how to raise children, how to raise teenagers."

Mark acknowledged that things were not always easy and that he recognized his need to talk with someone outside his family and friends. For example, he said, "I had no idea how to raise my own teenage children," but he was determined to change that. He gained an insight from an observation made by his counselor: "Your grandparents hired others to do their parenting, and that comes with wealth."

Early in Mark's adult life, he tried to bridge the gap between his father and himself. His first wife (who subsequently passed away) and their two boys would often travel to visit her parents. While his wife and the boys were away, Mark had a rare opportunity to spend time alone with his father.

His father had an illustrious legal career and arranged for Mark to work in the office next to his. They traveled together to work, but each engaged in his own business. Somewhere in the second or third year of this routine, Mark realized that he could spend four days with his dad and not once would his father ask him a question about his life. This crucial insight left Mark longing.

Later we will talk more about Mark and his father. For now, note that Mark made a considerable effort to change the kind of world he would create for his own children. For example, one aspect of his family history was recurring bouts with alcoholism; this was one thing Mark was anxious to change. He recalled the satisfying moment when his oldest son, many years ago, turned to him and said, "Thanks, Dad, for breaking the cycle with me."

While Mark's yearning to have a conversation with his father never went as far as he desired, he consciously made the effort to make a difference with his own family. It's definitely not magic!

Tale of Two Advisors

Unfortunately, we believe that an imaginary wall exists between our intangible longings and the actions we take to plan for our tangibles.

We once sat with a man who wished to buy property in upstate New York as a retreat for his family. He was very specific about the experience he wanted to create. So we turned to two advisors to get their input. The first immediately referred to the balance sheet, calculating the consequences to his portfolio. The second simply said, "I'll do whatever it takes to help him find the place, even if my team has to travel with him to find it."

Both advisors knew that the feasibility of buying the land needed to be considered. But the second advisor addressed the client's wish directly. He knew that if he wanted to help this client create lasting wealth, he needed to address the client's dreams, especially ones that centered on finding a way to connect across generations.

Our longing to pass on our wisdom (the intangibles) is universal. Mark Black's conscious effort with his own children and the popular reaction to the story of "Easy Eddie" demonstrate that many people share this desire and feel it deeply.

Of course, I wish my father could have said to me, "Jamie, let's talk about..." before he passed away. I suspect my father struggled with starting the conversation. Perhaps, like other parents, he was afraid of appearing controlling, or, like Mark Black, his relationship with his parents was operating behind the scenes.

Most of us know such conversations are not easy, so in the next chapter we will explore what makes them so difficult.

CHAPTER 3
The Legacy Dragons

Clearly it was a personal conversation, as the couple spoke in hushed tones. They were both dressed in black and looked visibly upset as they boarded the bus, taking a seat directly behind the driver. They talked quietly about returning to the house of mourning after the funeral. At first, I could only catch bits of their conversation, but soon their voices grew louder, until everyone on the bus had heard about "the brooch episode."

It began when they had walked into the house and saw family members opening every drawer, closet, and cabinet, as well as digging through purses. All were hunting for the cherished memento, a pin. As they scoured the house, they spontaneously shared memories of when it had been worn: "At my wedding." "On her 50th birthday." To each member of the family, it was a treasure. Ironically, this brooch was a piece of costume jewelry with little monetary worth, but it had immeasurable personal value.

In their grief, this couple on the bus gossiped about the peculiarities of the family members. They were astonished that the somber mood of the day had unexpectedly turned into a spectacle. It was as if I were listening to an audio book on my iPod. I was pulled into the mystery, listening for clues that revealed "what really mattered."

The commotion began when the middle sister was accused of taking the pin from the house when no one was looking. Confronted by the family, she asserted that it had been promised to her a long time ago. "Of course I took it," she said. "It's mine."

Remember: Our wisdom lives in the intangibles.

The oldest brother replied, "If it were truly yours, you wouldn't have tried to sneak it out of the house before the funeral." Obviously the dragons in this family wasted no time in coming to the surface. Abruptly, someone declared, "This is the end of our family, I've had it!"—and then vanished.

Within minutes, those paying their respects to the family found themselves standing alone in the house, uncertain about what to do.

Ready for a quiet bus ride, I sat back in my seat. What happened next was amazing. One by one other passengers chimed in with their stories. Soon the bus driver could no longer contain herself and declared, "You think that's bad, let me tell you what happened in my family!"

> **Think of a time in your life when you experienced a situation where the dragons took control.**

This story is universal. The names are different. The cherished possession is different. The setting is different. Yet in every situation, the dragons of jealousy, envy, greed, and power struggles take control.

Each of us enlists trusted advisors to help create plans, both financial and estate, to tame the dragons. But the nature of these dragons is to create chaos. They can't be controlled. Our plans merely force them into hiding. Then when no one is looking, they're positioned, ready to breathe fire.

We make plans for the quantifiable tangibles, such as money and cherished possessions. These are things we can touch. However, if our sole focus is on the tangibles, we give control to the ever-present dragons. The intangibles of guiding principles and beliefs, family tradition and culture, and life experiences should drive our decisions and help us manage those things that get in the way.

Tangibles without the intangibles creates an unbalanced legacy. Remember: our wisdom lives in the intangibles, and wisdom is an essential part of a balanced legacy.

Something Always Gets in the Way

Invariably, in life something gets in the way. Oftentimes it is more than a mere obstacle. To put it another way, life is a garden in which weeds, bugs, snails, and slugs are all minor nuisances and extremely destructive.

In relationships, these obstacles, these pests, appear dramatically as fire-breathing dragons. Their goal is to create turmoil. We know them. We have experienced their presence within our families and in organizations. We sense them lurking in the shadows, waiting.

When least expected, they appear. They seize the opportunity to make a situation more complicated, and they ruin relationships.

They boldly march in as challengers. Someone abruptly states, "I won't do that!" Or insists, "If you do that, I won't participate." Or demands, "Don't invite them, or I refuse to attend." Or, with authority, states, "I would never give my money over there; I'm going to give my money over here."

Disguised as family members, the dragons named Jealousy, Envy, Greed, and Power Struggles run the show. They are daunting and intimidating, and they taunt us to engage in battle.

Taking Action

To be effective in dealing with the dragons, a twofold response is required. First, it is necessary to acknowledge, whether we like it or not, that the dragons are always present. These feelings are part of human nature and are often what motivate people. Second, be thoughtful: tactfully manage the dragons.

Efforts to eliminate them put us off balance, which leaves us in precarious positions. By limiting our focus to trying to capture the dragons, we miss opportunities to build relationships, grow, and be innovative. As dragons are a constant presence, it is advantageous to manage them and keep them in their place.

Such challengers are a force to be reckoned with and must be addressed. Pretending they do not exist fails to neutralize them. To manage these divisive characters, it behooves us to understand what motivates them.

Wisdom is the key to managing the dragons.

Jealousy

Jealousy is the green-eyed monster. This challenger has a self-righteous nature and a single purpose. We usually associate jealousy with love triangles, yet in families, it appears in a variety of relationships. We must be alert to its destructive nature. From the safety of our couches, we watch our favorite TV soap opera, where jealousy provides much of the story's material. In real life, jealousy devours people, at least psychologically. As writer Michael Beer puts it, "Jealousy is a tiger that tears not only its prey but also its own raging heart."

* * *

The family was sitting around the dining-room table when Jeff got up to get dessert from the kitchen. His three sons had come with their families to visit for the holiday. Each had earned a professional degree—one was a medical doctor, another an attorney, and the third an accountant. Thinking their father was out of earshot, one brother looked at another and said, "You are so lucky that Mom and Dad gave you the down payment for a great house." When Jeff overheard the comment in the kitchen, he was startled. He and his wife believed they gave fairly and equally to each of their sons.

* * *

We know the dragon of jealousy is lurking when we see people upset about not getting what they believe is their fair share.

"Jealousy is a tiger that tears not only its prey but also its own raging heart."

— Michael Beer, author

Envy

Aristotle said, "Envy is pain at the good fortune of others." Envy spurs on competition; it is as if someone we'll never catch is running ahead of us. Those who are envious believe that without material possessions or a special skill, their uniqueness will go unrecognized. Their personal fears prevail. As a consequence, they perceive that their standing with family and friends is diminished. They accept that their rival has become triumphant.

Children in sports often experience envy. They see competitors as those who have superior skills to be able to win. Their trainers coach them to be the best they can be, to keep trying. They work hard to overcome their envy.

* * *

Eric worked hard with his father and grandfather to build a chain of hardware stores. As they grew up, Eric's three children worked with their father in one capacity or another. From the time his daughter, Susan, finished college, she held positions in various departments of the business. Her expertise was identifying new tools and gadgets. In contrast, when

"Envy is pain at the good fortune of others."

— Aristotle

her brother Gary was in college, he took a job in only one of the family hardware stores during the summers. Eventually he set out to become a lawyer, achieving partnership in a large law firm, outside the family business.

Eric is planning on slowing down and is grooming Susan to be president, so she can run the business. But Gary, in spite of his decision not to work in the family business, is envious. His response is subtle. It appears he is testing whether his father still loves him as much he does Susan. He recently asked his father for financial assistance so he could put an addition on his home.

Clearly Susan has both the skills and interest to run the chain of hardware stores. However, Gary feels as if he is worth less than his sister in the eyes of his father, even though he is a competent attorney, recognized in his field by his peers and family.

Greed

Greed is insatiable. "Earth provides enough to satisfy every man's need," said Indian philosopher and social activist

"Earth provides enough to satisfy every man's need, but not every man's greed."

— Mahatma Gandhi

Mahatma Gandhi, "but not every man's greed." The desire for wealth, power, or even food can be a driving force, especially when a benefit is denied or forbidden. Think of the motives of many villains in movies or plays, and how in comics, superheroes are enlisted to thwart the devious plans of the greedy. The greedy want no one else to have what they desire. At its core, greed is driven by narcissism.

* * *

Consider William, a trustee of the family estate. Even though he is given control of the family money, he feels he doesn't have enough. As a professional accountant, he earns a decent salary, and he receives a retainer from the trust. However, he looks at the investments and wants to have more than his siblings have. He cannot control his insatiable appetite, so he misappropriates holdings with the sole intent of building his personal funds.

Power Struggles

Power in relationships is about exerting a strong, direct influence over others. Naturally, each of us wants to influence family and friends. The problem is not

"You cannot rely on the traditional authoritarian model anymore. It does not work. No one wins in a power struggle. No one."

— Kitty Kelly, journalist

in the pursuit of power; it is in the intoxicating feelings that accompany power, which place barriers between people and harm close relationships.

American journalist Kitty Kelley once said, "You cannot rely on the traditional authoritarian model anymore. It does not work. No one wins in a power struggle. No one." And yet we constantly see the struggle for control between individuals and in families. The stakes are high for all, and everyone pulls, tugs, and strives to retain a sense of individuality and independence. In the midst of battle, it is hard to know whom to trust, and people start choosing sides. But in the end, no one wins.

* * *

This was the experience of Tracy, the eldest son appointed as sole trustee of his parents' trust. By nature, he is extremely conservative and feels obliged to manage the funds according to the wishes of his father. Even with the best of intentions, he is pulled into power struggles with his brother and sister. The terms of the trust require his approval for distributions. He and his family continue to participate in holiday dinners together, but he enjoys them less and less.

? Identify the strengths of each of your family members and those important to you.

Each of us is familiar with the strengths and weaknesses of our siblings, children, and close relatives. But it is a family member who is usually chosen as the trustee of our legacy. In an effort to be fair, we try to treat everyone equally, even though we know things are never really equal.

An attorney told us the story of what he calls the "forever trust." There was a mistrustful patriarch who wanted to preserve his legacy. Thus he created a special trust to protect his financial legacy from dissipation. Even though it was for the benefit of his family, the trust was tightly structured so that no family member could benefit from it for generations.

His effort to slay the dragons eventually backfired. The dragons became the guards. The family was prohibited access to the funds that continued to multiply. Eventually in a court battle, the family won control of the trust, gaining access to the funds so family members could benefit more quickly.

Yes, the dragons of jealousy, envy, greed, and power struggles are everywhere. When we recognize them, it is our wisdom that empowers us to manage them accordingly.

In most families, conversations about money and its impact are few and far between. In some families, the topic is completely taboo.

CHAPTER 4
The Myths of Wealth

Picture your family table. Look around. Notice who is sitting there. Imagine one empty chair at all your family meals. No one talks about that chair, yet it wields great power in the conversation. The chair represents money. A family secret!

Wealthy families have their own rules about keeping the secret. But let's not deceive ourselves: the empty chair could be found in anyone's home. We know it has been at our table. How about yours?

When guests arrive, everyone scurries to cover the chair. Over time, we realize that other families also have empty chairs. When we build up the nerve to ask a friend or acquaintance about his or her empty chair, the immediate response is a cautious nod of recognition. Suddenly we realize we are not alone. Our experience is more commonplace than we ever thought.

Over time we become familiar with the cautious nod. The vast majority of people we spoke with in preparing this book acknowledged that conversations about money and its impact were few and far between. In some families, the topic was completely taboo.

Intentional Legacy Planning

Most of us barely crack open the door to conversations about the empty chair. Advisors recognize that to be trusted, they must consciously navigate a path that allows their clients to be comfortable talking frankly about their wealth. They must address directly the dangers and opportunities affluence creates for future generations. Since engaging is critical, it is time to move beyond estate planning and begin intentional legacy planning.

This book is about the legacy conversation, and money is an essential component of the discussion. For clarity, we've drawn an imaginary line separating wealth as a cultural phenomenon from "my wealth," or more directly "my money."

In our society, we consider those who have acquired a certain amount of money or assets "wealthy." Personal perceptions color whether we see our families or ourselves as prosperous.

In reality, the cultural and personal aspects of prosperity are intertwined. But, for a moment, let's look at them independently and explore the myths associated with each of them.

Behind our cloaked approach to discussing money must be something frightening. Lurking behind the empty seat and waiting to strike are the sinister dragons. Since they are so threatening, we naturally avoid them. The dragons thwart open conversations even in situations where successful outcomes would calm everyone's fears. Creating, protecting, and growing wealth are not the best indicators that the dragons have been managed.

The Greatest Taboo: Sex or Money?

Sexuality on daytime soaps has opened the way to acts of passion being regularly seen on nighttime television. It was not that long ago when cultural standards required separate beds for couples on television, even if they were married. Portraying sex openly is now commonplace. For better or worse, sex is part of our everyday culture.

But is the same true when it comes to talking about our wealth and money?

Over thirty years ago, clients in our private therapy practice were reticent to talk about their sexual lives. Now such hesitation emerges only when asked about their family or personal wealth. Our queries are often met with silence; we see their discomfort about acknowledging their wealth. They are anxious about how they handle it.

Money Is the New Taboo

Recently a counselor shared with us a conversation he had with a client who was about to start counseling. The initial session involved discussing the fee. Without hesitating, the prospective client indicated that she could not afford it. Knowing she came from a prominent family, the counselor took a risk and asked about her financial resources, for it was clear by anyone's standards that she was wealthy. Affluence for her was not an opportunity; it had become an obstacle.

Conversely, entrepreneurs confidently share specifics about their financial situations. Those who started with little are especially likely to exhibit pride in what they have accumulated. They do not believe they are flaunting their affluence; they believe they have earned it. Passing on wealth requires the participation of everyone. Both those who have it and those who will receive it must be involved. Building stronger intergenerational relationships enhances everyone's ability to engage in real wealth planning.

Debunking myths and managing imminent dangers are the first steps.

Wealth Myth 1:
Wealth is THE Solution

One of the most wished-for antidotes to personal unhappiness is to become wealthy. The expression "money won't buy you

Money is the new taboo.

happiness" doesn't stop anyone from thinking that it will and wanting more.

Often we tell second-, third-, and fourth-generation wealth holders to "behave responsibly." We do this because we believe that unless they manage their wealth successfully, all will be lost. But this admonition often backfires. How easily the message turns into scolding. "You better be responsible! We all know you couldn't have created this wealth, and you probably don't deserve it."

A prominent attorney found himself serving as trustee of a former client's estate. Concerns about the youngest son had been a regular discussion with this client, who had also become a close personal friend.

After his father's death, the son approached the attorney to receive a distribution so he could open a business. What an awkward situation—the attorney wanted to honor his former friend's wishes while giving this young man a chance.

He gave the son a million dollars and encouraged him to use the money responsibly, warning him, "This will be your only chance." The young entrepreneur felt the pressure; if the business

You want the next generation to be accountable, but the odds are they will make mistakes. How will you encourage them to take responsibility while allowing them room to falter?

did not succeed, he understood he would forever be labeled irresponsible. No other words of wisdom were offered.

In his day, the father had made business mistakes along the way, but these were long forgotten. Building wealth for his family had required risks, perseverance, and even a couple of failed ideas. But for the son, failure was anticipated and equated with fiscal irresponsibility.

We assume that wealth is neutral. It's not what you have, but what you do with it.

Wealth Myth 2:
Wealth Taunts the Dragon

Those who have "great wealth" live with the fear that the external dragons will take control, destroying what past generations built. People warn them to be guarded, noting threats can come from such disparate sources as marital partners and new tax statutes. Shifts in the market, as well as changes in the leadership of a family firm, are two ways that make having wealth a risky business. It's important to differentiate between the need for thoughtful planning and an unhealthy preoccupation with every potential hazard.

Whether our wealth came easily or we struggled to obtain it, affluence connects directly to our sense of self. As a result, the possibility of losing everything is a constant threat.

Carolyn and I were once riding in an elevator carrying a booklet that had the words *Inheriting Wisdom* in plain sight. We were asked by other riders to share our elevator speech about wealth, and afterwards, they offered their solution: "Just spend it all before you die."

They heard none of what we said about passing on guiding principals, traditions, and life experience. Their ears perked up when we briefly mentioned connecting one's wisdom to one's worth, but as soon as they heard the comment about "one's worth," the dragons taunted them.

Each person in this group had come from meager circumstances and had done very well in life. The refrain they planned to tell their children was "No free rides." The lesson they took away from their own experiences was "You must earn it." They had deep fears about "trust-fund babies," and they believed that free money destroys initiative.

There is some truth to their fears and beliefs. Wealth can be dissipated over time, and our assets must be protected and managed. In addition, no one can argue with the horror stories of those who weren't prepared to handle money in productive ways. Yes, it's easy to see the weaknesses of those we have influenced, but at some point we can no longer serve as our families' protectors; they are in charge of their own lives.

Wealth Myth 3:
Too Much Wealth Is the Problem

Regardless of economic class, the doors to feeling shame seem wide open when it comes to money and financial status. Ironically, one can be ashamed of being rich as easily as being ashamed of being poor.

Early in our conversation with Mark Black, that fourth-generation descendent of a 100-year-old family business, he spoke about "optimal wealth." He shared his views: "In a general conceptual sense, there is an optimum level of wealth, beyond which increasing wealth brings some negative behaviors. Greed is something that grows with wealth; it's not satisfied by wealth."

We assume his conclusions came from personal experience—his life on the board of his family company and his expertise as a consultant in family business and governance.

By contrast, we assume that wealth is neutral. It's not what you have, but what you do with it. Unfortunately, people often believe that certain human qualities are associated with poverty, a middle-class existence, or wealth.

True Wealth

I never thought I'd be standing in this place. My grandfather, Benno Weiner, owned a mansion that had once stood on this empty corner in Dresden, Germany. As many other Germans had experienced, Allied bombs had destroyed his city and his home.

I ended up on that empty lot because several years earlier, my curiosity had been aroused when I received a call from a researcher. He was attempting to help Jewish families recover money for property that had been seized during the reign of the Third Reich. On my own quest, I set out to recover more than money for my family.

I relished the opportunity to regain my lost legacy. My grandfather, "Opa," had been something of a fictional character in my life. In 1939, my parents emigrated first to Palestine, then the United States. My paternal aunt and grandparents settled in London, England. I only saw my Opa's endearing smile in person a few times in my life. One vivid memory I have of Opa, when I visited London, is of him giving me a British pound. I used it to buy Matchbox® cars and toy soldiers.

I have come to learn that my grandfather was unique. My cousins in England grew up with him. They speak with admiration and affection about his personal qualities. My cousin Ronnie jokingly says, "He is *my* Opa, Jamie. I can't share him with you."

With assistance from the researcher, I began to discover my grandfather as a real person. He arrived in Dresden from Russia, but by the time he left Germany, he owned a department store with two branches and a clothing factory that employed over 300

> Does your family measure wealth in terms of acquired assets or accomplishments?

workers. My aunt reminisces about her life growing up with butlers and maids. Opa was considered wealthy.

In 1939, he was driven from his business and home in Dresden and made plans to join my aunt in London. While still in Dresden, he envisioned earning his living by opening boarding houses.

As the story goes, he sold his custom furniture to buy pieces more fitting for a boarding house. At the last moment, he stuffed his good jewelry in the legs of the furniture and headed to England. He was stopped at the border by a Nazi guard, who said, "We have heard that Jews have been known to hide jewelry in the legs of furniture." With a straight face, my grandfather replied, "I can't believe Jews would do that." Without examining a thing, the guard let him proceed.

Our family did recover a portion of the money that once belonged to my grandparents. But what is most significant to me was that moment I stood on the grounds where he once lived. It was then I knew he had brought great wealth—his wisdom—to the family.

CHAPTER 5
The Myths about Money

I remember walking through a department store when I was around 7 years old, seeing a toy I wanted, and immediately asking my mother to buy it for me. Of course, I no longer recall exactly what I wished for. Yet the memory of my mother saying, "Jamie, we can't afford it," remains as vivid as my childish response: "Well, just charge it!" I held the magical idea that a pot of gold existed somewhere.

So you can imagine my chuckle when I hear a young child in a store demand from her mother or father, "Get this for me!" followed by the childish command, "Just charge it!" Clearly the belief in an endless treasure is universal in our culture. Young children make no connection between money, desire, and reality.

Each of us wants to leave our mark on the world. Each of us has our own money story. Each of us seeks an individual path in the search for rewards, money, or recognition.

Each of us can remember the age we first learned some truths about money. There are those of us for whom the memory is clear; for others it is vague. We subtly learn our socioeconomic status long before we have any idea of the actual meaning of this term. However, by the age of 8 or 9, we have already accumulated experiences and stories about the impact of money on our lives.

Our culture connects designer labels with having money. Driving a foreign sports car gives us more status, especially when others know the price. Sales people, both men and women, decide which car to drive based on the impression they want to leave on clients. A comptroller told us her company provides a bonus for each partner so he or she could lease a prestigious automobile, and the company even encourages the partners to upgrade their cars with accessories. Creating the image of having money is paramount for many people. Money is equated with sex appeal, competence, and stature.

The media lauds those who were raised poor and yet, with persistence, created successful companies. We give accolades to those who faced obstacles and became self-reliant. Of course, the mistakes they made along the way are forgotten. Errors are considered the price of doing business. Our praise centers on their hard work and the bottom line.

Those raised in affluent families recognize at an early age that something is different about them. Although they wear the same brand of clothes as their friends, when they visit their homes, they notice glaring differences. These children hear stories about the founder of the family business. Passing hospital buildings, art museum collections, academic campuses, or religious institutions, they spot a plaque bearing the family name. But often, none of this is talked about openly.

Each of us wants to leave our mark on the world. Each of us has our own money story. Each of us seeks an individual path in the search for rewards, money, or recognition.

What makes finding our individual paths more complicated, however, is that our culture perpetuates many myths about money. As in *The Wizard of Oz*, these myths are illusions. They are designed to explain behaviors we observe, and to

Our culture perpetuates many myths about money... these myths are illusions.

address concerns we have about the consequences of those behaviors. But heed this warning: the myths set us on a path directed by fear and only encourage the dragons that seek to block our way.

Let's look at three myths about money that often cloud our perspective.

Money Myth 1:
There Is a Pot of Gold to Be Found

This myth professes that undetermined amounts of money will provide the happiness and acceptance we seek. Believers in this myth often fall hard. At some point, most people eventually realize that the pot of gold at the end of the rainbow can never be reached. But if you follow the promise of this myth, just watch the dragons rear their heads. The grief generated from believing in this misguided myth does not dissipate until victims free themselves from its hold.

How do you recognize and validate the initiative and hard work expended by family members, even those who do not receive awards and prizes?

Neil talks about his sons, Adam, 25, and Michael, 28. Adam was a star on the high school swimming team. He received a full college scholarship based on his talent. In high school, Michael was Adam's strongest supporter, even coaching him. Yet Michael always felt he was second best.

The elder son, however, is a whiz with numbers. Using his financial acumen, Michael began a logo T-shirt business in college. He graduated with honors, and several of the large investment firms vied to employ him. To this day, he continues to achieve great things in the financial world.

Neil, who would like to have grandchildren, is concerned that Michael has difficulty staying in romantic relationships because he's always running after the next big deal. When father and son are together, Michael often talks about wishing for a financial windfall, the one that will make it possible for him to settle down. Neil knows the recognition Michael is seeking will never be enough and will never be achieved by chasing the mythical pot of gold. Until, as Neil puts it, he "looks at himself in the mirror and accepts that what he is searching for is actually before him."

Money Myth 2:
One Must Suffer to Achieve

This myth is buried in punitive comments like, "Pull yourself up by your own bootstraps." It assumes the world is a dangerous place and we must protect ourselves against a myriad of hidden threats. This is the antithesis of believing in the pot of gold, in which life is full of possibilities. With this myth, hard work and success, rather than being the result of thoughtful, wise effort, turn into dragons that can never be satisfied.

Randi is in the midst of a divorce from her husband of twenty-five years. Davis, an attorney who worked his way up the ladder, is now the managing partner of a large law firm. Randi, who graduated from college with a nursing degree, has stayed at home raising their children, who are now in their late teens. Davis is filing for divorce and is only providing minimal financial support to Randi. Randi's parents are divorced also. When she asked for financial assistance, her father, a self-made man, told her to go out and get a job: "Just pull yourself up by your bootstraps. I paid for your education; use it."

Naturally, Randi is depressed; she has been out of the workforce for twenty years and is unsure of her skills and herself. Her worst fears are confirmed. She's convinced that she is alone in a threatening world, with no one to protect her or be there for her. She has essentially adopted her father's belief that she must struggle in order to achieve financial success.

Money Myth 3: "The Good Life"

Gail grew up comfortably in Indianapolis, Indiana. Like most of her friends, she went away to college. Wanting a profession, she earned an accounting degree. Then she set out to live in a place teeming with people, a place where she could make a name for herself. So she moved across the country to Los Angeles. Things went well for a long time. Gail had a good job, married a wonderful man, and had children. Then life happened. Her husband lost his job. Her company instituted a wage-and-hiring freeze. Gail and her family ended up moving back to her hometown, a comfortable, ordinary place.

In *The Wizard of Oz,* Dorothy runs away from her ordinary life in Kansas because she longs to be in a place "somewhere over the rainbow," far away, with no troubles. When the illusions surrounding the myths are exposed—as happened to Gail—it changes everything. When the myth is exposed as false, we are required to use our strengths and apply our personal wisdom to find a way to reach our objectives.

The goal of building wealth is to provide for future generations. It is about intentional legacy planning. When we manage the dragons, we are closer to fulfilling our hopes and wishes and empowering the next generation. No one should be paralyzed by fear.

Your Own Money Story

Many things influence the decisions we make when we are shown life's opportunities. Family messages influence the paths we choose, which can be professional, corporate, entrepreneurial, or the "couch potato" variety. Those messages about success focus on achievements, recognition, and financial com-

When the myth is exposed as false, we are required to use our strengths and apply our personal wisdom to find a way to reach our objectives.

pensation; this course sets the expectation to find employment that pays well (sometimes within the family business). When competitiveness is promoted, we strive to become the most popular or the wealthiest (or we just give up).

Yet there are those who disregard every message they hear and forge their own paths.

No matter the path, each decision and action we take is focused on growing our own garden and cultivating our seeds of wisdom. When we feel satisfied, then we can choose to connect it to others' gardens, like adjoining plots of land that make up a farm.

Ryan's family owns a farm in South Dakota that has been in the family for four generations. Historically, each patriarch or matriarch intentionally passes the ownership of the plots in a way that keeps the family farm connected. In the midst of writing his will, Ryan's father, Terry, informed him that he and his brother were to inherit the plots.

Ryan and his brother, Tom, have left the life of farming, left South Dakota, and have each achieved success in business. Each has made his own mark, using his own talent and abilities. But now Tom plans to return to manage the family enterprise. This surprised Ryan. Even though he is not planning to return to South Dakota or to farming, Ryan supports Tom's decision.

What path did you follow?

Terry recognized early on the importance of Tom and Ryan experiencing what it is like to follow their unique paths toward personal success. They needed to achieve some level of independence if they were ever to return as contributing adults in the family business.

Wisdom is able to debunk the myths about money and manage the dragons. We take a step closer to the family by finding our own voice as young adults. We learn. We discover. Then we bring back to the family our own story about money and become involved in maintaining family cohesion.

It is critical to bring together the intangible dimensions of our wisdom with the tangible spokes to develop a robust, lasting legacy.

CHAPTER 6
The *Inheriting Wisdom* Legacy Wheel

I t wasn't unexpected, but he still felt numb. Ben Baker stared into the phone, feeling like a character in the movies. Only this was real life. His father, George, 72 years young, had suffered his second stroke. (Ben and George are members of a composite family, which we will discuss more in the next chapter). Ben replayed the phone conversation in his mind. Then, to manage his nervousness, he mentally went through a personal checklist.

For the previous fifteen years, Ben had worked beside his father in the family real estate business. In 2004, the business was sold for a substantial amount. His responsibilities merely shifted from running the family business to running the business of the family. George remained involved, choosing Ben as his confidant. Following the sale, they spent hours with their advisors creating an extensive estate plan. Dealing with the family was a roller-coaster ride. Issues many of us face also concern the Bakers: medical crisis, divorce, substance abuse, stepchildren, and educational requests.

Although still in shock from the news of the second stroke, Ben wanted to assure himself that all the bases were covered. He and George had spent many hours in meetings with trusted advisors, thoughtfully planning for this day (of course, they believed it would be further in the future). Yes, there was a financial plan, so the family office would continue to run and make distributions. Yes, George and Ben had written wills, including well-constructed trusts. Yes, George had signed the necessary documents concerning medical treatment, including a medical power of attorney. Ben also had a good relationship with George's physicians. Recently they had begun working with a firm that specialized in creating strategies for philanthropic gifts and grants. Most of George's art collection was part of a trust. George was divorced, so the jewelry, china, and several family treasures were with Helen, his first wife.

Startled back into reality by the ring of his mobile phone, Ben heard from his siblings: "Why are you letting her take charge?" ("Her" was George's second wife, Gretchen, a nurse.) "I'm on the road and can't get to the hospital until tomorrow; let me know if anything happens."

This is not the way it was supposed to be, Ben thought. *We planned, yet something is missing.*

George was fortunate: he recovered from the second stroke. For Ben, this medical crisis had been handled, but it was clear to him that something more was needed than the plan they had worked so carefully to put together.

This book recognizes that fear exists for those who have money, as well as for those who are afraid of not having it. However, by this chapter, we've seen that we don't have to be paralyzed; we can manage the dragons. And we realize that our wisdom (our guiding principles, family traditions, and life experiences) is as important to address as the tangibles, such as money and cherished possessions. The intangibles vitalize and strengthen our intentional legacy.

The Legacy Conversation presents a unique approach to helping families discuss both the tangibles and the intangibles. Families are encouraged to discuss money, including exposing the false myths surrounding it—such as the assumption that there is a magic pot of gold. Personal exchanges are designed to reveal what actually makes these myths powerful. This promotes open communication with the next generation about the empty chair at the table, acknowledging and keeping the dragons at bay.

The intangibles vitalize and strengthen our intentional legacy.

We've emphasized the importance of engaging in cross-generational conversations. We prepare ourselves by understanding what is important to us, the first step. We have designed this book to help readers discover what is individually important, rather than offering a prescribed strategy for everyone. The stories we use, including our own, are designed to bring each of us closer to our own experience, to our own stories. The point is to discover the wisdom you want to pass along.

The next generation is growing up accustomed to many forms of interactive communication, such as Twitter®, Facebook®, YouTube®. These forums are participatory and facilitate social networking. *The Legacy Conversation* is also a helpful tool designed to begin interactive and meaningful communication.

The *Inheriting Wisdom* Legacy Wheel

We begin the process of passing on our wisdom by looking at where we are today. Taking purposeful action is the key. An intentional legacy plan is dynamic; it details steps you can take today (to get family members on board) and ones intended for the future.

It is clarity about the design of our intentional legacy plan that evades us. Naturally, there are things of which we are certain and want to include. However, passing on wisdom follows a path that is unfamiliar to most of us. To be effective, we need a tool that provides a structure.

The *Inheriting Wisdom* Legacy Wheel is the essential instrument for determining what is important to each of us, as this is personal. It provides clarity, while creating opportunities to reach across generations. The spokes of the wheel are structured to organize our unique wisdom and then forge a plan that engages those important to us.

A few words of advice when it comes to using this tool. Begin taking steps today. Take small ones. Action is what's important. Get comfortable talking about your wisdom. Engage those important to you. Avoid the tendency to rush ahead, take time to banter, to talk about your ideas.

Look at the Legacy Wheel. Observe the circular construction. Its design reminds us that our legacy is dynamic; it rolls along from generation to generation. Our lives, our wisdom, and our relationships are active. At times this is exhilarating, at times discouraging—the process is constantly in motion.

Passing on wisdom follows a path that is unfamiliar to most of us. To be effective, we need a tool that provides a structure.

The *Inheriting Wisdom* Legacy Wheel is composed of ten spokes. Notice how the wheel, which represents the spheres of meaning in our lives, is divided into the tangibles and the intangibles. These are two distinct and complementary arenas, which make the *Inheriting Wisdom* Legacy Wheel and the primary concerns of our lives a complete circle.

The five tangible spokes are: legal, philanthropy, medical, cherished possessions, and financial.

The tangible spokes are clear and definite. These are areas of our lives that we can measure. Often we seek trusted advisors to help us manage issues in those realms, creating plans for current and future uses. It is important to realize that the tangible spokes remain separated until they are connected by our wisdom.

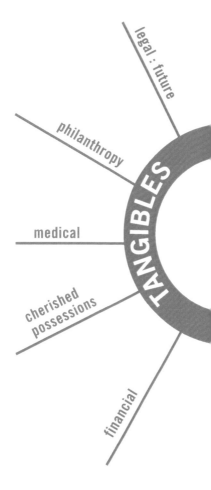

The *Inheriting Wisdom* Legacy W
© 2008 Adler & Forest, LLC

Ben and George Baker worked with their advisors to create the necessary documents for each tangible spoke. But when the family had to deal with the patriarch's stroke, the dragons emerged from hiding. Ben recognized his responsibility, which seemed overwhelming. He realized that there was an estate plan, but not an intentional legacy plan.

Our wisdom lives and grows in the five intangible spokes: family culture and traditions, spirituality, well-being, accomplishments, and guiding principles and beliefs.

For each of us, wisdom is unique and personal; it is found in each spoke. It forms the basis for our decisions, whether we are consciously aware of it or not. This reality is often not articulated, but it is central to our thoughts when planning. We constantly use insights acquired from family and life experiences.

To develop a robust, lasting legacy, it is critical to bring together the intangible dimensions of our wisdom and the tangible spokes. They are seldom connected in planning, but it is our wisdom held within the intangible spokes that guides and informs the decisions we make in tangible arenas. The questions trusted advisors ask us require succinct answers, but our thoughts and reasoning are more subtle and intricate.

To incorporate our wisdom, it is critical to start our legacy-planning process by articulating our thoughts and dreams. When considering what is important to us personally, it is the questions we ask and the answers we give ourselves that are the first step. Action is what is important, even if it seems small. Remember, we begin where we are today.

That First Conversation

Again, engaging family members is high on our agenda. Open and collaborative conversations are the basis for building connections. To get things in motion, we take a step. Oftentimes, this makes us uncomfortable, because we don't know how others will react.

Passing on our wisdom requires us to stretch and reach across generations. Follow these steps:

Look closely at the Legacy Wheel. Reflect on your life experiences—positive events, adventures, and even ones that were disastrous. Choose one that your family may be unaware of. Consider a time that was disappointing, when feelings of shame were strong, or a positive one, when your action benefitted another.

After recalling the experience, think back to the situation. Mentally collect as many details about it as you can: the time, the people present, and the feelings you experienced.

Pause. Take a breath.

Next, identify the challenge presented to you by what was happening. Perhaps it was a problem that required your input into the solution or an uncomfortable situation you thoughtfully handled. Perhaps you had to answer to a parent. Perhaps you wanted to avoid embarrassing a family member. Perhaps you had trouble meeting someone's expectation.

Open and collaborative conversations are the basis for building connections.

Then recall what you did. How did you handle the situation?

Now you have a story that contains a piece of wisdom.

This is a way to begin a meaningful conversation with the next generation. Share your story, and as you do so, encourage the others present to join in and tell their stories.

The *Inheriting Wisdom* Legacy Wheel incorporates our intangibles with the more obvious tangibles. Our wisdom and our wealth are intertwined. Conversations with the next generation about our knowledge and insights are critical. Such an exchange creates a robust dialogue and allows us to pass along our wealth meaningfully and wisely. That in turn will enable the next generation to thrive in rapidly changing times.

Start to create your intentional legacy plan—today.

CHAPTER 7
The Baker Story

The description of the training program for Classic Pastry Arts from the French Culinary Institute's website suggests that in six to nine months you will be able to:

"Learn breathtaking skills, including conquering the tricky chemistry of chocolate, theatrical sugar skills, and beautiful, fanciful presentations" (www.frenchculinary.com). Making pastry is an art form. But few families, if any, end up as well crafted and flawless as the creations of a master pastry chef.

The same institute offers a program on the Art of International Bread Baking. In a much shorter time, eight weeks, "you'll build an impressive repertoire that includes breads from Italy, Germany, and France." Bread-making is a craft.

We'd like to introduce you to the Baker family. They are our concoction. You've already met George and Ben in the last chapter, but now we'll describe the family in more detail. Families are not created with the same precision as fine pastry or with the same attention that goes into the making of elegant breads. But despite their imperfections, families do hold together—at least as well as pastries or breads.

I recently sampled some outstanding chocolate chip cookies. As the batter was being made, the cook discovered she had forgotten to buy chocolate chips. A scavenger hunt that scoured every corner of the kitchen produced all kinds of chocolate from many different sources (leftover candy bars, toffee). Little bits of all this chocolate served in the place of store-bought chips. The result was amazing.

In a similar fashion, we created the Bakers from morsels brought to us over years of professional experience as psychologists. No one individual story makes up this portrayal; in fact, we've seen each element of the Bakers in many different families. Readers will recognize something about themselves and their families somewhere in the Bakers' story.

Making pastry is an art form. But few families, if any, end up as well crafted and flawless as the creations of a master pastry chef.

Most people have an image of how they want their lives to look. So when the reality does not meet their expectation, they turn to psychologists like us and ask us to "fix it." Often they want us to make their lives be like the finest pastry—flawless.

We've created the Bakers to pose an alternative: to create a way to help make family life better through engaging conversations that improve the way they:

- *Support the dreams and ambitions of family members*
- *Strengthen connections so that everyone can reach across intergenerational barriers and build stronger bridges*
- *Use both tangible and intangible wealth to increase the enjoyment and prosperity of the family and its members*

Long ago, and even today in some cultures, marriages were arranged as the first step in legacy planning. One family would agree to a suitable union in exchange for a tangible (land, dowry, alliance), with clear hopes that the marriage would ultimately increase both estates.

In most of the world today, in response to the forces of love and individual choice, we count on chemistry to bring two souls together. We expect these unions to rise to the occasion, just like baker's yeast. Unfortunately, the ideal conditions don't always exist, so the results of these mergers vary greatly.

Families never start with a perfect match, whether arranged or drawn together by chemistry. We count on love as if it were magic glue. But if our bond is similar to "the chemistry of chocolate," it is not likely to stick. Only when we actively dedicate ourselves to sustaining love can we expect it to hold together over time.

Whatever our dreams, when we conceive or adopt children, we discover that temperament, as well as environment, influence their personalities. Life has a way of taking over. Nothing is as first we imagined it. There is so much in our rapidly changing world that has an impact on our families, both from within our homes and from without. Then our offspring grow up and start the process all over again. Sooner or later, they bring strangers home. Hopefully, we accept these new faces and call them family.

In spite of, or maybe because of, their flaws, families hold together. Ill-chosen ingredients, terrible timing, and lack of control may not produce elegant outcomes, but families endure no matter the recipe used to put them together.

The Bakers are okay, as families go. But they do have their "stuff." We made sure they had more than their share. Creative cooks often do brilliant things with the random fixings they find in their kitchens. Television offers shows where chefs are challenged with outlandish

Only when we actively dedicate ourselves to sustaining love can we expect it to hold together over time.

ingredients in order to test who can be the most masterful.

For many of us, cooking at home includes using leftovers before they spoil and leave us with unwelcome odors. So we create, perhaps a stew, and enjoy.

Unfortunately, most of us tend to avoid problems until something stinks or is about to turn bad. For the Baker family, it's not too late to deal with their "stuff." With an intentional effort, they have the chance to bring out the best in one another and savor what they have created. Human beings have unusual resources to open communication and move into action.

Open and collaborative conversations are the basis for building connections.

We've already seen the outlines of what the Bakers' mess looks like, but let's fill in the color.

Commander in Chief

Living in a patriarchal world, it's no surprise that at 72, George Baker still exerts tremendous influence over his family. We should remember that his ability to call the shots and take risks allowed him to start his real estate development firm in the first place. Since the formation of his business

> **Families endure imperfections. Identify several imperfections with which you have chosen to cope.**

in 1965, taking charge has worked pretty well for him.

Ben, the second oldest son, who currently runs the family office, has determined that George's net worth is at least $50 million. Being of a generation that kept their cards close to their chests, particularly in terms of finances, we are not surprised that no one truly knows the entire picture. Speculation exists that George's holdings could even be as much as $120 million. In George's mind, the assets are his. Even though the family holds meetings, everyone knows that the final decisions rest with George.

When he was 24 years old, George married Helen. Over the years, she did everything for George. She was responsible for the house, their social calendar, and, of course, the family. After all these years, she thought her life was settled.

Then, in 2004, George developed serious health issues. Helen found herself in the position where she needed to confront George, particularly about the management of his health. This was tough on both of them.

Without consulting anyone, George arrived at a family gathering and announced that he had sold the family business. No one was prepared for what followed.

Such a Disappointment

Many years earlier, Michael, who is now 48, believed he was heir apparent. Athletic and charming, he became responsible for what, at the time, was the lifeblood of the business—sales. At the height of the housing boom, sales was the easiest part of the family business. During those years, Michael often came into conflict with Ben, his brother, who had taken on primary responsibility for the actual development of properties. Michael would make promises to prospective buyers, and Ben would have to figure out how to deliver.

A couple of years before the sale of the business, Michael's life turned upside down. His wife divorced him. While no one raised the issue, the family knew he abused alcohol. Everyone excused their avoidance of the obvious by noting that Michael was still functioning and pulling his weight, but barely.

Feeling pushed out, Michael left the family business and found a sales position in another company, where he continued to do well financially. At the time of the divorce, his twin daughters were already off to college. Since they were not living at home, it was easier for them to maintain a connection with their dad.

The "Good" Son

Ben, who is 46 years old, moved firmly into his role as the "good" son. Married to Nadine, they have a son named Zachery. Ben's job over the last few years has been to preserve the assets that came from the sale of the family business. Nadine is actively involved in charity work. Their biggest concern is that Zach seems disinterested, not only in the family's affairs but in much of anything. No one is certain whether this is a product of being 19 years old or a response to other family factors. Zach does well in school and doesn't get into much trouble, so they feel they have little leverage to engage him with the family.

While we never can undo the messes we have created, we can find ways around them. We just need to be careful of the dragons.

The Dam Breaks

George, who could accept Michael's drinking problem, was torn apart when his daughter, Joyce, showed up with her partner Elaine. He found this situation totally unacceptable. When they began to talk about adopting a child from overseas, George left the table. Joyce is an attorney, and Elaine has money of her own, but adopting a child is still expensive.

George's health began to decline in 2004, but everything changed when he had a stroke in 2005. Helen could no longer care for George's every need. Enter Gretchen, his nurse, occupational therapist, and, eventually, his second wife. She is 45 years old, the same generation as George and

Helen's children. And she has a son who is the age of George and Helen's grandchildren.

Gretchen's son, David, is a "wild child" who is indulged by his father and, according to his mother, uncontrollable. Gretchen turns to George to create an incentive trust to straighten David out.

In the meantime, Ben can no longer figure out how to keep being the "good" son as he deals with the demands and expectations of family members while he manages the assets. Everyone is troubled by the situation.

The Gift of Imperfection

Pastries and breads are at their best when fresh from the oven. In contrast, families have the opportunity to improve on their imperfections at any point in the process, even using them for the greater good.

Of course, people can step so far over the line that those around them can never risk trusting them again. But as long as families can find enough safety to use two of our greatest tools, then even though life will never be perfect, great things can be accomplished. This makes us unique.

On which spoke of the *Inheriting Wisdom* Legacy Wheel would your family connect?

The two tools are good conversations and meaningful action.

While we never can undo the messes we have created, we can find ways around them. We just need to be careful of the dragons. And the longing for a different outcome, the desire to have an impact, must outweigh our preoccupation with our hurt feelings.

Just imagine what would happen if the Baker family had used these tools. First, after all the years of George's control, they'd have to make sure that each individual's wisdom is at least recognized. The *Inheriting Wisdom* Legacy Wheel discussion would turn out differently for each family member.

They would eventually find some overlap between their spokes, hopefully enough to be able to develop a plan together. But it's easy to be drawn back into old patterns—you know, it's those dragons.

For all of us, including the Bakers, the key is to find ways to continue to live the plan. Remember: love involves dynamic action; it's not static. For each family, this process looks a little different.

CHAPTER 8
The Power of Legacy

"Thanks, Dad, for breaking the cycle!"

What more could anyone ask than to hear unsolicited appreciation from one's children, given privately, of course. Testimony from the next generation is the greatest honor we can receive. Whether biological, adopted, or acquired through marriage, our children are our future.

The story of Mark Black mentioned in an earlier chapter, a fourth-generation family executive of a 100-year-old company, illustrates that devotion is neither a miraculous moment like Easy Eddie's, nor a heroic action like that of Butch O'Hare's. Mark's devotion reflects a deeper longing. Because of his actions, the world will be left a better place.

Drawing upon lessons he had learned in life, Mark shared with us his struggle to be approachable as a father. (Many details of Mark's story, including the identity of the people, have been changed.) When his children became adolescents, he recognized that he had no idea how to raise them. In discussing his concerns with us, he made a connection to his own life, the source of his fears. He had been a "visitor at home, starting at the age of 14." Like his dad, he "had no idea how to raise teenagers." Mark observed that often one of the untoward effects of wealth is being estranged from parents. Boarding schools and caregivers can provide the best education and give some supervision, but they don't build a connection with parents.

Imagine the path between Mark's apprehension about raising teenagers and his son's words years later. For us, his experience serves as a reminder of our capacity to use our imperfections and create something amazing.

Mark's focus was on raising his children. Having two older boys when his daughter was born, he often shared with others his intention to be "an imperfect model for my children" so that he could embody direction and standards, yet be accessible and fallible—"a work in progress" in their eyes.

For us his experience serves as a reminder of our capacity to use our imperfections and create something amazing.

Perhaps Mark's strength as a father was his conscious desire not to cover up his vulnerabilities. He believed that his children would benefit from seeing him as approachable. Most of all, he wanted to make sure his children would not end up feeling that "they are less than their father." At the same time, he knew it was important that they see him not only as a man with direction, but as an inspiration for being decent husbands and fathers themselves.

Widowed for seven years, he met a wonderful woman and remarried. He laughs as he says, "Business people would say I 'acquired' a daughter in the transaction." Mark put in the effort necessary to make sure he had a "terrific" relationship with his step-daughter.

In describing the teenage years of his children, Mark admits that "the connection got thin sometimes, but it never was broken." When his children each reached the age of 20, Mark felt he could let go of the sense of responsibility he had for them as his children and become their best ally.

Mark used his business experience to bring a passion for seeking renewal to his

Mark's strength as a father was his conscious desire not to cover up his vulnerabilities.

own family. Even when his first wife passed away, he found a way, over time, to revitalize his life and thus, his family.

Everybody Should Own a Widget Company

Since the sale of U.S. Widgets, Mark has taken time to reflect on his years of service on the corporate board. Given who he is, Mark stayed on the path of revitalization and re-created himself professionally.

Mark often quotes his younger brother: "Every family ought to have a widget company. It's just nice to have a widget company in the family." He jests with us, "Wouldn't you like to have a widget company in your family?"

Mark recognizes that few family firms last for over 100 years. The desire to maintain a reputation for business integrity and product quality has guided the company from Day One. As a fiscally conservative firm, the company expanded beyond its roots, using its own money to build new factories. It is amazing what can be produced over a 100-year time span.

It's unlikely that Seth Black, who founded the company in the early 1900s as an equal-equity owner with his brother Ralph, could have foreseen where the company was headed. Nor could either of them have predicted that, after a four-hour meeting and a handshake agreement, the board would sell the firm for $3 billion. While that day marked an end point, for Mark, a new life phase with different challenges began.

Organizational renewal has been one of Mark's longstanding interests. Prior to going on the board of directors of U.S. Widgets, he was employed by a technology company. Mark's focus was to help businesses find a competitive advantage in the market. As we noted in an earlier chapter, Mark likes to say, "I am always at my peak when I'm in a steep learning curve."

When Mark joined the company board, he replaced his father as the sole family member from his great-grandfather Ralph's side of the family. During his tenure on the board, he witnessed its transformation.

At the beginning, the board's role was primarily a perfunctory "rubber stamp" for management, but in response to a need for change, the board began supplying active oversight of the business. Mark was able to become a dynamic participant in that change process. He came to the board with an interest in change, and the experience placed him in the "grand theater" of a big company that knew it needed to overhaul how it did business. Renewal has been an ongoing theme for Mark, both in the world of business and in his personal life.

From Floral Arrangements to Family Engagement

Mark recalls the days when most family shareholders were passive owners, attending the annual meeting but otherwise not involved with the business. While the meetings were formally conducted, there was always a friendly competition for the floral centerpiece at each lunch table. Mark commented, "I competed for the floral arrangement because I knew my wife (who was at home taking care of the kids, a four-hour drive away) would be happy to see me come home with such lovely flowers."

After the sale of the family business, Mark wanted to figure out a new path to pursue, one that would make him more independent. Revitalizing his business interests, he started by becoming an active participant in a volunteer organization, whose mission is to support business development. He built a platform utilizing his experience with boards.

In the years that followed, Mark put together seminars and tailored governance practices for family businesses throughout the country. Whenever he can, he tells his story. Passion, experience, and determination have been combined to support his work with family-owned firms.

Eventually, Mark started his own firm for his family and their interests. He notes, "My insight is on how important it is to look a generation ahead, and we are looking at my children and my cousin's children."

No Stranger to the Dragons

Mark discussed his efforts to involve his generation of the family. He noted that only in the last forty years has a conscious effort been made to help affluent families sustain family cohesion and their wealth. He noted that the Rockefellers were among the first to organize their family operations. In contrast to his years of passive participation and competing for flower arrangements, Mark finds excitement at the prospect for active involvement.

Of course, Mark is no stranger to the dragons that get in the way of families. We suspect that this was part of what drew him to learn about family governance. Meeting hundreds of families, Mark observed the potential that existed for producing better results. After all, a learning, growing environment has always been the world in which he thrives.

Mark never referred directly to the dragons in our conversation, but his account of the family dynamics within U.S. Widgets indicated that they were lurking behind the scenes. It was apparent that Mark knew the feelings that arise in families are to be expected. He chose not to focus on family horror stories. His interest has always been figuring out what could have worked better.

Mark knew that the roles of the two families who founded the company were different from Day One. Seth Black had been the central figure in the development and subsequent history of the company. Timing played a big part, since Mark's great-grandfather, Ralph, passed away within the first few years of the launch of the business. Ralph was significantly older than his brother and financed the start-up. The differences between families were fertile ground for negative feelings (the dragons).

Whether families have means or not, opportunities and rewards are never equal. As simple as it seems, the number of offspring or grandchildren on either side of a family alters the outcome. In this case, the descendants of Seth Black consisted of few members, while Ralph Black had over thirty heirs. Using simple math, one side had access to greater wealth per person.

Mark's immediate family did not escape the effects of jealousy, envy, greed, and power struggles that surface in most families. Whatever Mark has been through over the years, he neither complained nor used his experiences as an excuse for inaction. His approach to life is proactive.

Considering all the variables in family firms, Mark appreciates what it takes to sustain and grow a business over a century. As we talked, it was obvious that he had come to accept what he couldn't change. His choice was to actively work to bring value where he could.

"I Admired My Dad's Career!"

Professionally, Mark admired his father's accomplishments. During our conversation, it was apparent that many of Mark's professional strengths were similar to those of his father.

With an undergraduate degree in British History, dad had gone to Yale University and Yale Law School. Mark believes that early on, his father made three great career moves that distinguished him. Having specialized in maritime law, his father became fluent in Norwegian and quite capable in French as well. This opened the way to personalizing client relations as Europeans were inclined to do. Mark admired him for building these relationships.

Mark's father also found his way to the top of the International Maritime Law Association by developing an expertise in bills of lading, a topic of interest at every conference. A bill of lading is the piece of paper tied to the ownership of the cargo, which is bought and sold like a security. While this was not a specialty that others desired, the company really needed someone with expertise.

Then Mark's father started a mentorship program within his law firm, bringing young Scandinavian law-school graduates in for 18 months of training. A generation later, these law students had become the ministers of the seas and general counsel to big ship owners. By that example, Mark gained an appreciation for what it means to develop deep client relationships.

Mark's admiration of his father, who spent his whole career in a law firm formed in 1935, extended to his language capacity for French and Norwegian. He recognized his father's interest in British history was all part of what made him an unusual man, one worthy of respect.

His father's law firm had power of attorney for the Norwegian Merchant Marine in World War II, assigning him the full legal right to make decisions for the Norwegian merchant fleet during the time when Norway was under threat of Nazi invasion.

Mark wished to be an approachable father and devoted himself to creating a different dialogue with the next generation.

The Son of a Lawyer

Despite his admiration for his father's accomplishments, Mark felt his father suffered socially. "He was great with words and little quips that played with the meaning of words and so forth.... He never could speak a word of what may have been most important." His father never had casual male friends, ate dinner separately from his children, and appeared to keep most of his conversation with Mark's mother focused on the politics among the partners in his law firm. Mark longed for deep conversation, which his father found difficult to offer him.

Mark intentionally "broke the chain" with his children. We know that breaking the chain means more than changing a particular behavior. Mark wished to be an approachable father and devoted himself to creating a different dialogue with the next generation.

For all of us, the challenge is to keep the conversation going and to move into action as families, to participate together. The first step is to initiate the conversation. Let's get started!

CHAPTER 9
How to Start Your Conversation

Every Expedition Begins with the First Step

Your legacy conversation is a journey—with a beginning, a few stops and restarts, and (if done consistently) a successful outcome. However, embarking on the course, having that first exchange, takes bravery. That is because your legacy plan carries heavy emotional freight.

Oftentimes, you put off discussing legacy issues, as lurking dragons are daunting. You are concerned and fearful. You don't want your family frayed by greed, jealousy, envy, or power struggles. Then there is your trepidation about being misunderstood (no one wants to be derided). The scary conversation is put off...until a more opportune time.

In our experience, knowing is always better than imagining.

Skye, a young woman in her mid 20's, told us about her grandfather. In his 20's, Fred immigrated to the United States, married, had four children and worked hard. From Skye's perspective he was focused, clear in his wisdom, and gruff. Skye was the youngest grandchild of the brood. Even though the family gathered every Sunday, she believed that her grandfather barely noticed her. She had many imagined conversations with him where he expressed disappointment in her actions and life choices. Then one day she decided to really talk with him.

She began by expressing her gratitude for all he had done for her and her appreciation for the opportunities he afforded her. Then she steeled herself for his tirade listing her flaws, as that was his style. Much to her amazement, he told her how proud he was of her and that he thought she was one of the "most caring people he knew."

In many cases, an imagined "let's talk" is worse than what actually occurs. Ninety percent of the time, when you sit down to converse face-to-face, an initially awkward

Knowing is always better than imagining.

The Legacy Conversation

chat begins to flow. The exchange is far more satisfying and less disturbing than your nightmare. Yes, the dragons lie in wait. Your advantage is that you are prepared, poised for a response if they get too close.

Instead of remaining immobilized by fear, acknowledge the dragons and their tendency to create chaos. Then imagine the seemingly unbearable conversation and how it will play out. Role-play the conversation in your mind, including the other person's worst response—anger, disappointment, or incredulousness. Imagine your various replies. Now you are ready for the actual conversation.

As you well know, they seldom go as you plan, or as you have rehearsed. When feeling off balance, allow yourself to pause as you get your bearings. The key to reaching your goal is to continue trying. Be persistent.

Live History...Make It Come Alive

Of course any journey comes with risk. But consider that the greater risk is standing still.

How often have you remarked or thought, "I wish I had said...," after a family gathering, wedding, funeral or phone conversation? An opportunity to connect is missed. You are left with an empty feeling.

Moments fly by. Life is not forever.

My vivacious aunt Fern is in her 80's, and still dances up a storm at family weddings. Her grandson, Andy, was visiting us from England. Over dinner we talked about her rich history and his close relationship with her. Ellen, his fiancé, commented that their future children would not really know her. Capturing Fern's vitality and stories was the key to preserving her history.

We encouraged Andy to dedicate time and regularly have conversations with her about her life, recording it any way he chose. To reach his goal, he created a schedule and an outline as a personal road map. Over the course of a year, he collected stories and pictures, discovering new relatives along the way. At Fern's 83rd birthday party, Andy presented a beautiful book to her and the family. Fern's legacy is now in the present and future. It will speak to generations to come.

Family videos are an engaging way of preserving the essence of family members. Colleen was in charge of coordinating a family gathering for her parent's 50th wedding anniversary. Unexpectedly her father, who was in his 80's, became gravely ill. This delayed the celebration to the following year when, thankfully, he was in better health. She felt a sense of urgency to capture the stories and wisdom of her parents as soon as possible.

Colleen took a deck of *Inheriting Wisdom*™ Conversation Starters and distributed them to each family member present, from the youngest, age 6, to the oldest. Then she sat her parents in a place of honor, surrounded by their children and grandchildren. Colleen turned on the video camera and recorded the exchange as the children asked the question on their card, and her parents told their stories. There was sharing, active listening, and one grumpy aunt even smiled. Soon the videotape was full. But the family was still deep in conversation. Everyone was present in the present.

One of the risks of avoiding having legacy conversations is that the next generation is left unprepared and under-engaged in the future of the family. For anyone to put 'skin in the game,' they need to be an active part of the family. Engaging in intergenerational conversations creates an atmosphere of affirmation and guidance through successes and failures.

The legacy conversation starts with your curiosity.

The Conversation Starts with Curiosity

Expressing sincere interest in the people you value and love is the most effective starting point. By doing this, you dismantle the imaginary wall that exists between your intangible longings and the actions required to plan for the tangibles.

Let curiosity be your guide. Be genuine as you explore what is important to the other person. Your goal is to build a relationship based on commonalities, while recognizing that identified differences can co-exist. A cautionary word: it is critical that you avoid confrontational questions about wealth when starting your legacy conversation, as they immediately put the other person on the defensive.

Conversations create an opportunity for sharing.

Open the door for sharing wisdom, guiding principles, traditions and life experience, as you make room for each generation to fully participate.

Preserving and Protecting the Family

You start with a conversation. Keep in mind this is only the beginning. Over time, any awkwardness and stiltedness that accompany your discomfort disappear, and conversations about the intangibles and tangibles become commonplace.

Regular and meaningful conversations encourage your family to acquire an open mind-set. An expanded perspective of family members develops through these discussions. Relationships are built or strengthened. This leads to family collaboration, cooperation and wholeness.

Begin with Preparation

First, just as you would do for any important event, prepare. Thoughtfully consider the tone you want to create. Sharing is personal and brings people together. Rather than lecture, use these three key principles to create a bi-directional exchange, one where each person contributes.

1. *Assume that everyone has wisdom.* Each of us possesses inner resourcefulness; wisdom. Incorporating this outlook helps you convey openness in your demeanor and voice quality. Remember: wisdom is central to how we live our lives. Although the age and number of life experiences of each person differs, everyone can contribute to the conversation.

2. *Everyone wants to be heard.* Next, acknowledge the universal desire to be heard. This positions you to listen carefully rather than thinking about what you are going to say next. Remember: you can listen. Even if you disagree with what is being said, just keep your thoughts private, until the timing is right.

3. *Acknowledge that it takes time for the message to be fully processed.* Conversations are an exchange of words and ideas that live in our thoughts long after the cup of coffee is finished. Our lives have

Although the age and number of life experiences of each person differs, everyone can contribute to the conversation.

a rhythm, which can be smooth or choppy. One thing that complicates communication is the pace of life; our tempo and that of the person we are talking with are oftentimes different. We may be ready and geared up, but the other person may be distracted. If unacknowledged, this leads to a discordant exchange. Therefore, it is crucial to take this into account.

Acknowledge the universal desire to be heard. This positions you to listen carefully rather than thinking about what you are going to say next.

We live in a world that affords us instant connections. What are often missing in the words of an instant response, however, are a depth and breadth of meaning. You know what you want to say; allow time for it to be revealed.

Your ability to connect on a personal level is enhanced by remembering these principles. Pause and say them to yourself. Your mind-set is an advantage. It enables you to manage the lurking dragons.

Now you are ready.

The Conversation Itself

Ask About the Day

Begin the conversation with a request. The authenticity of your inquiry can be detected, so be genuine. Say something like, "Tell me one good thing that happened to you in the last forty-eight hours."

It sounds simple. Sometimes the other person may even think it is a trick question. However, it conveys an interest. It sets the tone. It keeps the dragons at bay.

Ask for Stories

"When you first began your career, where did you think it would lead?" Or, "I'm curious about how you succeeded." Or, "I've always wanted to know more about what you want for me and the next generation." These types of questions honor each person's life experience, by focusing on that which is important to each of you. Thus you open the pathway to an exchange of wisdom through the exploration of the failures and the successes within each story.

Share a Story

Share a story you read in the newspaper, or something that just happened. Then connect it to yourself. Engage the next generation as you discuss it. Encourage them to tell about an experience, a situation, or event of which they are aware.

The process is often initially awkward. But time is to your advantage. Keep the lines of communication open. Consider keeping a journal where you record your thoughts, tracking the growth and development of the relationships that are important to you.

Send a Note

Stories are often told around the dinner table. You hear them at parties or when you spend time with a friend or family member. People will describe a situation, often filled with emotion, and then like a reporter tell how it was resolved or ended.

Comment on how they handled the matter and how it illustrates an effective way to manage the dragons. An observation might be: "Choosing to remain quiet kept you from being pulled into the chaos." Or, "Your comment about focusing on what really matters was insightful." When you do this, you encourage the conversation's focus to be about wisdom.

In addition, you can write a short note to the person, commenting on the wisdom he or she used to manage a situation. Consider handwriting a note, as it personalizes your message and allows you to be more thoughtful.

Given your personal style, which suggestion seems the best way for you to start today?

The Direct Approach

Arrange a family meal or meeting. Talk about the importance of wisdom. You can choose to share only your wisdom, or you can engage the other family members. At the appropriate time, introduce the dragons. Consider telling the "brooch episode" we mentioned in chapter 3.

Use the *Inheriting Wisdom* Legacy Wheel

Use the *Inheriting Wisdom* Legacy Wheel on pages 58-59 as a guide. From the ten spokes, choose two that are important to you. Or captivate a family member by discussing a spoke that appeals to them. The identified spoke serves as a starting point for your conversation.

Families grow as they learn about and appreciate one another's unique perspectives and talents. A legacy conversation conveys the importance of preserving and protecting the family wealth, as well as preserving and protecting the family.

This is about having a conversation. Find your personal style. We know it takes time. Start with a small step today.

This is about having a conversation. Find your personal style. We know it takes time. Start with a small step today.

Your Intentional Legacy Plan Begins With You

Remember: it only takes two people to converse; another person and you. Working together provides the setting. The activity can be fun or have a serious tone. You take a leadership role and guide others when you initiate a conversation.

Creating an intentional legacy plan requires sustained effort over time. The investment is worth it. Conversations turn into dialogues, involving advisors in the process and engaging family members. The potential benefit for the family is huge. Plans for how to give, how to invest, and how to encourage the dreams and ambitions of family members will take time. It is important that everyone has a say in the outcome.

When Expert Advice Is a Must

There are times when a family wants extra help to navigate their journey. We created *Inheriting Wisdom* and wrote this book because we realize how important this conversation is, and we missed the opportunity with our own parents.

As much as we love our relatives and think we can manage the legacy conversation, still there are dragons that can devour any family, even ours. We have worked hard to use *Inheriting Wisdom* with our family, knowing conversations can be derailed or worse, relationships ended. It helps to have the advice of an expert. Anyone can benefit.

> **When you started these conversations in the past, what method worked best?**

With the right assistance, you'll be able to design the next steps for your family—perhaps following a route you never imagined.

A guided experience is fun. Imagine carving out time for a family retreat or family vacation with a purpose. We have created a positive self-discovery experience for families. It is a systematic process that defines your family's wisdom as you identify ways to manage the dragons. You create your unique legacy road map.

It is the intentionality of your legacy plan that makes a difference—discover. create. your meaningful legacy.

A GUIDE TO READING
The Legacy Conversation

To enhance your reading of *The Legacy Conversation*, this reader's guide presents you with thought provoking questions. Journaling your response and ideas are a way to start your personal discussion. Selecting a question to share with your family or those important to you is a pathway to beginning a dialogue.

Another way to utilize this guide is to form a reading group and discuss the questions with your friends, or members of your house of worship.

CHAPTER 1
Your Legacy and What Really Matters

1. If your parents have already passed away, what regrets do you have regarding knowing more about them? If your parents are still alive, do you have a desire to hear their stories? Do you have favorites? Are there stories you would like to know more about?

2. Do you agree that the intangible part of your legacy is "what matters" in legacy planning? Why or why not?

3. Do you believe it's important to be intentional about your legacy, or would you rather it take care of itself?

4. What tangible asset do you want to be sure to pass on? What intangible? Is there an overlap?

5. Intangibles; thoughts, ideas, are often difficult to articulate. Is that the case for you? If so, why?

6. Consider the regret you may experience if you don't share your wisdom. If these ideas are important to you, consider writing them out first and then sharing them with those important to you. Learn about their wisdom.

7. What steps will you need to take to create an intentional legacy?

CHAPTER 2
A Deeper Longing

1. What gardens do you hope your heirs will sow and reap? Do you want them to tend your garden, or create their own? Why?

2. Consider your life story: highs, lows, and significant moments in between. If your life story were told, what would the common themes be? What parts do you want to make sure are heard?

3. If your parents were not intentional about passing on their legacy, consider why. Do you hold back in the same way? What effort will you put forth to pass on your legacy differently?

4. What proportion of your planning focuses on the tangibles versus intangibles? Why?

CHAPTER 3
The Legacy Dragons

1. Re-read the story "the brooch episode," that opens Chapter 3. Have you ever witnessed or been part of a similar scenario? What were your gut and rational responses?

2. Think of a time in your life when you experienced a situation where the dragons (jealousy, envy, greed and power struggles) took control. What prompted the dragons to come out?

3. In your family, what dragons show up most often? Why these specific dragons?

4. How have dragons ruined or debilitated relationships in your family? What part do you play?

5. Why do you think dragons appear when we least expect them?

6. What is the difference between defeating and managing dragons? Is one less productive? How?

7. What ideas do you have for tactfully managing your family dragons?

CHAPTER 4
The Myths of Wealth

1. If the "empty chair" in your family is money, what are you avoiding?

2. Why do we—and sometimes our wealth advisors—use an indirect approach when discussing wealth? What are the dangers of this communication style?

3. Do you agree that money is the new taboo topic? Why or why not?

4. Re-read the three myths on pages 36-40. Which one do you embrace? If not one of those, do you have another?

5. How do you define true wealth? How do you think your children identify it?

6. How will you encourage your heirs to take responsibility? Will you allow them to stumble? To fail?

CHAPTER 5
The Myths about Money

1. What new cultural beliefs about money are most disturbing to you? What does your family believe?

2. Do you have an immediate reaction to any of the three myths found on pages 46-49? If so, describe.

3. How do you recognize and validate the initiative and hard work expended by all family members, not just those who receive awards and prizes?

4. One myth about money that the authors highlight is that "one must suffer to achieve." Deep down, do you believe this to be true? Do you believe your children ought to "work hard" for their own wealth?

5. What wisdom do you have to debunk these myths? Write them out first, then have a conversation with your family.

CHAPTER 6
The *Inheriting Wisdom* Legacy Wheel

1. What may have held you back in the past from sharing your personal story and actively planning your legacy? What steps towards sharing can you use today?

2. Look at the ten spokes of the *Inheriting Wisdom* Legacy Wheel on pages 58-59. Which of these spokes do you feel you have addressed adequately? Which ones haven't you covered? Why?

3. The Legacy Wheel reflects a balance between documents and wisdom. Are you document heavy and wisdom light? Is this because of advice you've been given, or another reason? Is this a new concept to you?

4. Pick one spoke, then begin a conversation around this topic. What story or wisdom are you excited to pass on? Why?

5. In conversations with those important to you, what specifics do you need to be aware of for your chat to go well? What can you do to ensure that it's a collaborative and not a one-sided discussion?

CHAPTER 7
The Baker Story

1. What realities of passing on your legacy aren't matching your hopes?

2. Imagine your family and how it will grow and evolve if you engage in collaborative conversations. Paint the picture with words. How does this make you think or feel? Does it propel you to move forward and initiate more conversations?

3. The authors state that each family and its members have foibles. Do you agree? Do you see the reality of this statement in your family?

4. All families have strengths. Identify one or two in your family and discuss the benefits.

5. Why do families stick together when things aren't perfect? When do some families fall apart?

6. On which spoke of the *Inheriting Wisdom* Legacy Wheel would your family connect?

CHAPTER 8
The Power of Legacy

1. The chapter begins with Mark Black stating he "broke a family cycle." Are there any family cycles you would like to see ended in your lifetime?

2. What have you overheard about yourself that did or may motivate you to continue passing on the intangibles of your legacy?

3. Do you believe, like the authors, that we have the capacity to use our imperfections to create something amazing? Consider your imperfections; how can these be used to build something spectacular in your family?

4. What are the dangers of focusing on family horror stories? What might be a better focus?

CHAPTER 9
How to Start Your Conversation

1. Relationships are often heavily influenced by assumptions, as in Skye's story in the opening of Chapter 9. Does this scenario exist in your family?

2. All families have a myth or legend in their history. Who are the two or three family members with the most 'knowledge' about it? If you were to stage a family forum to explore the myth, what would that look like? Where might it lead?

3. How would an intentional legacy plan help your family distribute its tangible assets more strategically?

4. What "experts" do you think would help your family establish a clear legacy plan?

5. When do you plan to start your conversation with those important to you?

To deepen your legacy conversation, start by participating in the first two workshops that comprise the discovery phase of *Inheriting Wisdom's* interactive process. Begin by clarifying your wisdom: your guiding principles, traditions and life experiences. Rarely do any of us set aside time to clarify what really matters.

Next, you focus on building bridges between generations. You prepare yourself to manage the dragons of jealousy, envy, greed and power struggles that reside in all families. As the generations align, your foundation for a comprehensive legacy plan is set.

The aim is for you to live the plan during your lifetime. The action phase utilizes your clarity and intergenerational connection to link your wisdom to your worth. By incorporating the expertise of your trusted advisors, you create a holistic legacy plan.

Inheriting Wisdom is a specialty consulting firm focused on legacy strategy. It is "what matters" to your family enterprise and the individual members that is central. Your family wisdom provides the foundation for the creation of an intentional legacy plan. Thus, all members are empowered to pass on their wealth with meaning and purpose.

Please call us at 866-571-9648 or visit our website to learn how we can respond to your family's unique requirements.

www.inheritingwisdom.com

Be Forewarned:

These *Inheriting Wisdom* Conversation Starters stimulate engaging conversation with thought-provoking questions. They get things going. They are so much fun, you may spend far more time playing with them than you planned!

Based upon the *Inheriting Wisdom* Legacy Wheel (pages 58-59), the questions start people talking, sharing and chatting about "what really matters." Each 52-card deck is divided into seven categories, plus four wild cards.

To order your deck, call 866-571-9648 or visit our store at: www.inheritingwisdom.com.

Any journey comes with risk.
However, consider that by standing still the risk is greater.